Rhinoceros in Clumber Park

Also by Roger Craik

I Simply Stared

Roger Craik

Rhinoceros in Clumber Park

Rhinoceros in Clumber Park
ISBN 1 74027 207 2

Cover by W.A. Craik (with Albrecht Dürer)

First published 2003 by
GINNINDERRA PRESS
PO Box 53 Charnwood ACT 2615
www.ginninderrapress.com.au

Contents

For Laurie

Halloween Bucket in Lake Erie

That fall,
The year the skyscrapers blew up
And everything began to slide, grow weird and
Preternaturally mild,
I tore off all my days to walk upon
The unexceptional stretch
Of grass, stones, dusty littered shingle where
America gives out.

I'd seen its kind before, of course,
In orange rictus-baring rows
But here was one who'd said to hell
With Halloween and all its sickly freight, had tossed with one great shake
Its brains clean out of its skull, had spurned
Its sluggard fellows' landlubberly ways
To bounce and bounce its bumptious pumpkin face
Ridiculous atop the pewter waves.

Vulgar it was. And yet
How keenly I longed for that black serrated smile
To turn, like a broken lighthouse beam, itself again
On me, standing lost, on the edge
Of America that fall
The skyscrapers blew up and everything grew
Weird and weirder still,
And a silly bucket chose that day to bob and dance before it fell
To listing, sinking, never to be seen again, the happy thing,
Now smiling indestructible at sand and rocks
Through darkened centuries to come.

Day Trip

The minibus
Went jolting down indifferent roads.

The countryside, I recollect,
Was very green. I saw some cows.

The place itself
Looked exactly like the photographs

But spread surprisingly large:
The area of thirty football fields.

The sun blazed down
Upon the railway lines.

The air was full of butterflies
I'd never seen in Ohio.

I tried
From what I'd read and knew

To make such huts that stood, unrazed,
Hold thousands bunked in close putrescent dark;

To make the corridor
Of knotty rust-enfeebled wire

Volt-charged again
And then to feel, as they did…

But I failed. At ease, at large, I simply strolled.
It was a very sunny afternoon.

The air was full of butterflies
I'd never seen in Ohio.

June, 1956

Ten days after I was born,
Sylvia Plath and Ted Hughes married
In a London church

While I slept on, an amiable child,
Or was walked by my father in my large perambulator,
Smiled my first smiles,

Then grew up in an unexceptional
Midlands street, stroked our cat and other cats,
Splashed in a paddling pool.

And only now, when almost fifty years have passed
And my parents are divorced
And I am edging middle age,

I think of them, both now dead,
Marrying that Saturday
Then striding down a pathway lined with graves

Into a dusty street when everything
Beneath a London sky as wide as ignorance
Was whetted sharp by love.

Alone on Thanksgiving Morning

On the day that all the world had died,
Standing on my front door step
With coffee in a dark blue mug I bought
In Hartford, at some wordy conference,
I idly pressed my bell

And caught
In that ding-dong hackneyed chime
The sound that suddenly meant you,
The one you must each time have faintly heard through wood
Before the hurtling urgency of me inside,
Summoned by banality that I
Alone can recognise
As blasphemously you, uniquely you,
So freshly newly you each time, bringing your immeasurable
Gift
Of yourself

Which has me capering
While in my living room my samovar
Waltzes my candlesticks dizzy,
And on the floor my Turkish carpet undulates
Like some exotic deep-sea ray.

And there I'd be,
In one great sweep all fingers fumbling off your wedding ring
And smoothing with my palms
Your long black coat away to hang it up among
The jingling uncooperative triangles of wire,
And kissing every nearest bit of you, no matter what,
And helter-skelter tumbling out
My questions, telling you
All the things that I presumed
Of interest in my dreary day

So far

Until you came
And pressed the bell
And made me happy

Then.

Alone, of course,
Again and again
I press my bell

And every time, although it's not
– Although my reason tells me that it's not –

It's you, it's you, it's always always you.

The Model

Before the dullish mirror bolted firm
Upon the pastel wall, she contemplates
The body wholly hers at last, undressed,
And scrutinises one by one and then,
Together for their full effect, her breasts
Unmagnified by prying high-power zoom.
This week it's Tel Aviv: Manhattan next.

Fifteen floors below, the car horns blare.
Room service came and went. She sips a beer,
Surveys herself again. She doesn't sport
The cultivated sultry lip-curled sneer
That drives men wild, she's told, and made
Her somewhat famous, so she hears. Instead
She eyes her father in the fullness of

That mouth, and in the stare that, slightly cruel,
Reminds her of the office in Lahore,
Pistachios in a copper bowl, the phone
That rang and rang upon his desk, ignored,
The fingers swarthy round the heavy glass,
The hawkers' cries outside, and then the hush
As dusk became ornate with minarets.

How stale it all became, so soon! How scattered,
Dulled, she feels, how altered now from when
Her schoolfriends envied her the jet-set whirl
Of limousines and suites and cocktail bars
Where drinks were always on the house. She hums
A line or two from Paul McCartney's song
'Another Day', and sees, twelve hours away

Beyond the customs wall a pacing man
Whose avoirdupois fingers will arrange
The sand next day to trickle crystalline
Between her thighs so bronzed, so taut, so trim,
So unalive. She sighs. She wonders if
At twenty-eight, when at the corners of
Her glossy pout the lines begin to draw

The character that no one's ever thought
To get to know... And suddenly, as though
She'd walked out of a frowsty room into
A village street of sun-warmed twilight air
Giving way to stone-strewn roads that led
Through cornfields pricked with poppies, bursts the mood
For 1920s jazz, King Oliver,

The boisterous breaking-out, the push and pull
Of notes so brassy-crisp, each one about
Its busyness of joy. Her foot begins
To tap tap tap and soon she's capering,
Her beer a-tilt, inventing scraps of lines
In nonsense random French, remembering
The curtains billowing like sails into

The downstairs cottage rooms, and how the wind
Those girlhood summers blew the sea inland,
Resinous with pines. Again she longs,
Fifteen floors above a noisy street,
For garlic singing in the pan, and knows
The loss of meals no waiter ever brought,
Obsequious, but those she'd make herself:

The innocence of scrambled eggs, the toast
That jumped up merry from its silver box,
The coffee gurgling at its own concerns
Of being made, one sunbeam slanting long…
She looks around the room. Still life. The phone
Unringing by the tundra of her bed,
King-size, the two small lamps above, the phone…

The air conditioning begins to hum.

And Guest

The pleasant woman
With the daughters, undergraduates,
Invites my circumstances
And me
To dinner on Christmas Eve.

Hours, days perhaps, before I'm there,
The explanation will have taken place:

He's English, alone at Christmas.
No. Atheist, if anything.
You'll love his accent.
Can you believe he hasn't got a TV?

And now for hours across
Television's yelp and squawk,
I watch them watching, waiting for
My circumstances to arrive
While only I am here, alone.

Chapbooks

'No point in chapbooks' (so says George,
Well into his second beer);
'They're where good poems go to die.'
I wonder if that line is his.
It's much too rhythmical for George Bilgere
Who tells me that he much prefers
'The counterpoint of unmusicality.'
You can't get more unmusical than that,
And furthermore,
If a thing be through and through unmusical,
To what, pray, can it serve as counterpoint?

Now let me get this straight: a chapbook is
A kind of knacker's yard where thoroughbreds
(But only thoroughbreds, no wormy nags
Or frolicsome long-odds no-hopers, never placed)
Stand one moment firm of hock, renowned, mature, but past their prime,
And then are glue the next.

I question everything, and have for years,
Or so I tell myself.
Do I, though? Is it questioning, or something else
That gives my neighing flippancy full rein
To canter, caper, fetch its frisks at large
And then, abruptly, pulls it back at whim
To have it caracole, tittup, or preeningly piaffe
When at the very moment I am writing this, perhaps,
In some small house the next-of-kin
Are sadly going through the drawers and find
A stapled pamphlet, yellowing,
With her name on the front?
'These must have been some poems that Mom wrote.
I never knew she wrote – did you?
What shall we do with them?'
The other shakes her head, looks around the altered room,
Then reaches out her hand to hold
This casing of a life that's gone,
A tiny shroud.

There

'You recognise this,' he roared at me,
My xenophobic departmental chair
(Whom privately I called The Lion),
Showing around an American:
'It's your period, so you ought.'

So again I scrutinised the print
As I'd been doing every day I came in
Early for my class at half past eight
When the cleaners would be busy sprinkling
Water on the grimy floor, distributing
The dirt,
And thought again the things I'd always thought:

Twentieth century, during the war, perhaps,
Around the time of Gertler who went mad.
He can't do hands, whoever drew
Those two boys (or are they boys?) beneath
The one taut draught-admitting sheet. Papery, the fingers
Taper, fold like bookmarks. The nostrils, though,
('Nosethirls' as my father always said),
Scoured all night by light-bulb glare,
Exert themselves to hollow out the walnut shells of nose
That jut, like bone, above
The heavy lines of mouths ajar.
He paints, I think, the sound of snores.

However, I said none of this
But simply trailed behind,
Donkey-dumb,

And heard the bullying voice boom on
As if mere volume could atone
For this shabby corridor, the lights
That didn't work, the tea men smoking on the quiet, let alone
His 'doctorate' of summary and borrowings
Published as two hundred rough-grained sheets
By the in-house press, two buildings down.

Some other time I'll tell you how
Everything that year went sour, and how
In fear of order-barking green-felt-capped police I spent
My last five nights on different floors until
The only airline operating flew me out.
I watched for thirteen hours the tiny speck
Of plane that jerked its way across a screen:
Istanbul, Brussels, and, at last, New York.

The strainless hours spread into years.
I bought myself bone china mugs, CDs
Of Edward Elgar, Harry Partch, began
To cultivate a style I thought I'd lost.
I told myself I must not make a myth
Or demonise, or make a drama of
The past. And so, intently,
Using different words each time, I plainly told
The truth as I remembered it:
The woman upstairs being raped while I
Lay horrified and thrilled beneath;

The students bearing bribes, or gifts, or both;
The chalk that squeaked, and then would skid
Across the board, my fingernail juddering behind;
My telephone that gave two clicks and then would spread
Into a clumsy atmospheric eavesdropping.
They can't do anything, *anything* right.
But to be fair
(And here my tone, despite myself, would turn
Theatrically over-reasonable)
How marvellous it was to stroll at dawn
Around the amphitheatre and to feel
The gradual warming of the ancient stone
So open to the sky and sun. The land, the very land
Seemed old. My back against some massive palm,
Pistachios and wine at hand
And swallows giving way to pipistrelles,
Assuaged by evening's deepening blue I'd watch
The lanterns of the fishing boats that twitched
Across the darkening bay.

My recitations thickened into layers
Of retrospective guilt
Impersonating honesty.
I did not realise
That memory is not remembering
Until, leafing through a book for something else,
I stumbled across the sleeping boys:

Red and Green Sleepers. Henry Moore. 1941.

Then – Jesus Christ – he must have thought,
The stupid fascist must, astoundingly – get this –
Have thought the snoring lads were chimney sweeps by Blake!
Christ alive, that means he must have thought
(And must still think because he never reads a book –
Or can't, more like)
That Blake is sixteenth century!
At once the insights cut, with sudden pain, as when a razor scar,
Thin and tracing-paper white
From just above the eye
Down to the chin,
Splits open down a harmless old man's face
And beads the crimson blood afresh upon
The cheek his long-dead mother used to kiss.

Bastard.

Teaching Elie Wiesel's *Night* in Ohio

Someone sneezes, whereupon
Five others in full voice
Bless the sneezer.

I carry on,
Noticing in passing how His absence
Governs the subjunctive, cliché now.

I'm used to this.

Book and pad crash to the floor.
I'm also used to this.
It's not their fault the desks are small.

A performance, though, gets made
Of picking them up.
Someone mentions a movie.

And suddenly too calm to be annoyed,
Abandoned to the trawl and catch and swell
Of talk that must be life to them,
I just lean back, imagining
A long white empty stretch of beach,
Its inch-deep water warm all day
To splash and paddle in
And never think of thought, or past, or pain.

After the Interview

The interview over, in the suit
It took an afternoon to buy, you find
Yourself back in the altered corridor

Of the college where you teach,
Adjunct. It's 2.19 –
A nothing of a time.

As you strive to isolate
The strangeness of this afternoon
Abruptly made your own,

You see, beyond the doors' aluminium,
The late-spring lawn spread emerald,
With crowns of dandelions:

But not for long. Insensibly you're drawn
To where the car, hearse-black,
The second car you bought with him,

Waits statutory.
Already as you're going through
The rituals of seatbelt, smoothing-down and key,

You hear, three hours ahead,
A reasonable man, cross-legged, ask
The questions that you know he'll ask...

But suddenly
As everything begins
To move at different speeds

You all at once remember how,
As a schoolgirl, thirteen years ago,
You were allowed, even then to your surprise,

To walk across the town astir
With weekday unfamiliarity.
You saw

Its cafes, banks and record stores
Opening as you dawdled past
Taking every now and then

A few steps backwards, just for fun,
Or talking scraps of nonsense to yourself
Or running to some smash hit song

In spurts
Whose power you felt but did not know.
But now

The vision, questions and the questioners
Are gone, and leave
Your lecture orphaned on the empty seat

And roads unseen on either side that lead
To roads
And roads

And other roads.

'One girl there was'

Someone must have called the small girl's name
And she at once stood up and in one movement strode
Straight to the piano and began to play.

I don't remember what she played
Or if she won, or if I ever knew –
Only that some forty years ago

Whereas the others paused when their turn came,
Composed themselves, breathed deep, upon the stool,
As they were doubtless schooled to do,

One girl there was who rose and strode on stage to strike the keys
As if the music, just the music, were the thing,
Not all of us around not mattering.

Self-Delight

Underfoot the ancient stone is warm
In the temple where he strolls
At sunrise, glowing in the air
Of isolation. He's already seen
First a heron,
And then, a little later on, a lizard scuttling,
At his tread, into a crevice.
Also he happened to think of Matisse
And pondered how he might,
When he got back to his London house,
Buy a book of his drawings, savour them
Of a morning, over coffee, languidly, alone.
It's the economy he likes:
The sensual economy of line.

But you, asleep, know none of this.
You'll think it love when he returns to trace
The curve your spine makes, and to kiss
You into wakefulness. With him so close
How can you guess the dangers yet to come
On this and other mornings left to you,
From curve, recondite word, or scent,
Or cat that over thirty years ago
Would in his childhood's garden fetch its frisks
While the willow leaves kept rustling?

Perhaps you'll never know,
And years from now will sadly muse
How false it was, his love,
And yet so strangely true.

Epitaph

If last time you came you left a stone
Upon my grave, and this time find it gone –
Kicked off, you guess, into the unmown grass –
Or if, to your distress, the jar that reads
Frank Cooper's Thick-Cut Oxford Marmalade
Has spilled its flowers that, shrivelled up, lie strewn
Beneath the legend you had carved of me
Against your own mistrust, remember this:

The grave that you presume of me now serves
For couples clutching twenty minutes' life
From daytime's strip-lit falsifying hours,
Or for the pensive child who likes the stones,
Who rather likes the dead, as I did once,
And friendless wanders through these tussocked plots
And learns, although he does not know he learns,
A private catechism chronicled
Of names and dates and middle names
And four lines at the most of mundane verse
And things that people said a person did
Within a short and agitated space
Between two massive walls of nothingness.

But most of all it stands here for the boy
In blazer, shirt and regulation tie
Who, fleeing from the school gate's iron-tongued clang
Reverberating through his arm and spine,
Hurtles headlong, full tilt at my stone
And leapfrogs over by his fingertips
As if by jumping he could leave the earth
And fly, exuberant, beyond the sun.

My Mannered Hand

Richly dressing-gowned and breakfasted,
And staring over coffee at my lake,
I intimate in black decisive ink
My magisterial demands. The sun
Slants just the way I want it to across
The leather empire of my father's desk,
Beatifying pipe rack, paperweight,
Three soft lead pencils in a pewter jug,
An ashtray, paper clips, an ammonite.

It pleases me to muse that in due course
Others must perforce, *perforce* I say
(Savouring the near-forgotten word),
Exert themselves within a two-hour space
At talent's furthest stretch. Ah well. But I,
At ease, lean back, abstractedly to watch,
As if it were not mine, my mannered hand
Direct across the page the massy nib.
'Discuss, by means of close analysis...'

I sometimes wonder whether, in my day,
Back at the House, Jack Lewis used to look
With scorn at me, unpolished to his mind,
Just as now I cast an eye askance
Towards the spike-haired savages who slouch,
Their headphones round their necks, and chew, and spill
Their unthumbed unconned books as if success
Were theirs by right, by virtue of their youth.
Could I have been to him as they to me?

Such questions enervate. They're not my style
And that won't do. Instead, as usual,
I'll set intelligence to justify
The sophistry that serves my cause. A trick,
I know, just as it is to recognise
The ploy as honesty, and thus… Enough.
Besides, I'm finished now. High time to stow
The blotted paper in my drawer, and pack
Into the haversack I've used for years

A sandwich lunch and Plutarch's *Lives*, then dress,
And make the day my own by striking out
Beside the still canal. The heron waits
Attentive in the water flags. Perhaps
I'll see a rat beside the water's edge,
Furtive, pleasing, at his own concerns
While I'm at mine. I'll relish, later on,
The quieter pleasures, when the evening comes,
Of watching candlelight in darkening rooms.

On Listening to Prison Songs from Parchman Farm, 1947–48

(for Terry Cavanagh)

Their hoes strike down upon the stone-strewn earth
And once again one voice swirls up like dust,
And all the others join. 'Now *this* is art,'
I said, 'There's nothing precious or rehearsed.
The spontaneity's the thing, the rough
And readiness: the music *is* the work.
Perhaps they sang this one song twenty times
A day, these men, to keep themselves alive.'

'But these are felons, murderers,' you said.

First Journey

As inch by inch the train pulled out
With me inside alone,
I saw my mother in her fifties skirt
And black-rimmed glasses and dark coat
Watching still,
And then, as if to race the train,
My father running after me
Not as an athlete would
Or fathers of my friends at school,
But stroking, pressing down the air
With the heels of his hands and then with his palms
Like some great cat with padded paws.

And all that afternoon through hours of fields
And towns whose names lodge with me still,
I saw him in my mind's eye running thus
Beyond the platform's end and then beside the rails
On stony ground, on straggling grass,
Outdistanced, and outdistanced further still.

Proctoring, December 2000

I'm reading *Granta*, thinking to myself
Of a small blue pack of French cigarettes
Neat as genius
On some rainy afternoon
Redolent of vegetation and the earth,
With weeks and weeks ahead of me.

While my students write their last exam
And while I'm pondering in sub-Yeats vein
If I in my day were ever like them,
A man stands up, walks to my desk, and says,
'I don't need to worry about getting divorced no more –
My wife just died.'
And then sits down, goes on writing.

America.

Staedtler Mars Flexible Curve 24-inch

I

'Flexible curves contain
A square metal core
Coated with resistant plastic

And feature special edges –
One for use with pencils,
The other for use
With technical pens.

They are instantly adjustable
And retain their shape
Without support.'

II

So this is what it is and how it's made.
But even the least imaginative child
Would stretch his hand towards this blue snake coiled
Inviting, bright through case of celluloid,
Uniquely him to bend which way he will,
And name, and be the envy of his friends
But which, he hears distraught, is not a toy
But more (the teaching voice grows lofty here)
An aid, a help for grown-up engineers
And those who need to draw a perfect curve.

In forty years I've never felt the urge
With stick in sand or finger on light snow
On someone's windshield, least of all upon
A block of paper greyly meshed in squares
As drear as wire upon the Berlin Wall,
To draw a curve that's smooth beyond reproach.
Again I muse how little changed I am.
Always I've loved what's odd, or fugitive:
The Borealis or the weak marsh fires
Whose errant flickers ridicule the glare
Of steady symmetry that dulls our taste
And blinds us to ourselves. Now in my hands
And now around my wrist or on my desk
There coils this bright blue snake that's shed
Its name and, free of graphs and engineers,
Prehensile to my will, at last is mine.

Tonic Water in Cracow Market Square

Thin glass: lemon, ice,
Bubble-congregated straw
Corrugated at the rim.

'Cubist, accidentally,'
My education has me think,
Deep ensconced in wicker chair.

And later on
Perhaps I'll buy a Polish pipe,
Long-stemmed, of greenish wood, unusually dark.

But for now
It pleases me
To watch the pigeons, watch the crowds

An hour by train
From Birkenau.

Tutorial Advice

'If you're heartbroken, get down on your knees'
(She'd counsel women undergraduates
Unwise enough to ask for sympathy)
'And scrub the floor: it always worked for me.'

How fortunate for them they never saw
Her fretting through the frowsty listless days,
The telephone unringing hour by hour,
Grime slowly darkening the kitchen floor.

Beyond Reach

She, because she loved me, nailed black bags
Into the tree trunks, where they sprouted flowers
From hidden razored slits. She must have thought
I'd like to see them blooming there
When I returned from overseas.

But all I did was muse unworthily
Of Nature's tastelessness when in excess,
Of grafted stocks, of Spenser's Bower of Bliss.

I won't rehearse our breaking up, or things
That neither of us should have said, but did.
I only wonder how those gaudy flowers,
Long since tossed away beyond the reach
Of Nature or of Art to keep them kitsch,
Perturb me now as never then,
Even though I'm happier alone,
And writing this.

Minority Writer (1611–60)

Sir Thomas Urquhart, who is not Kate Chopin,
And who was not, because he was a man, repressed
By the patriarchal male-dominated society
Of seventeenth century Britain,
And who was not Hispanic but a Scot,
And who never wrote of the inner city (there not being one to write of)
And who, furthermore, far from being ahead of his time,
Was resolutely behind it,
And who told about himself enormous lies
And who is unknown to spellchecks,
Is thought of daily
(Out of the world's population of however many billions)
By one or two people,
I should think,
At best.

Long may he thrive, I say.
Long may he thrive!

Screen Weariness

When on my screen the self-styled cybersluts
Are pecking out those tired old misspelled words,
And bleariness is overcoming lust,
I think of you, van Gogh,
Who in a self-torn life found time to paint
Your sunlit wooden room at Arles
Where all a man need do is lie
Upon his single bed, alone
Beneath the many-coloured coverlets
To muse to sleep upon a whirl of stars
Until the greys and streaks of morning come.

Mornings

The leather of my father's desk
Basks taut, uncreaking in the sun's first splash
Before the screens and telephones begin.

Against the speed that rushes for itself
And squanders now for what might come,
How sobering it is to muse again

That in a few more centuries, perhaps,
The sun will slant where once wide windows were
And this great work-worn desk, and hand still young,

And no one left alive to read this poem.

Lines for Ann Who

Perhaps they needed the space
For somebody or something else,
And nobody had come with flowers for years.

And so the old slate graves were broken up,
Propped against a tree.

The fragment I retrieved,
Chipped from a smallish slab,
Is just

A left-hand border,
Fluting, curves,

And then two hand-heeled chiselled words
That carved another century's light
Into the dressed impassive grey:

Ann
Who

The rest
Is smashed away: the break
Shears off

Any mollifying 'e' there might have been
Of

Ann
Who

But does not spare
The known inevitable thing she did
That carves itself into
The living air
Just two feet distant from

My strangely moving disembodied hand.

Conversations with my Grandfather

Four miles was really far too much
For a small boy such as me to walk,
But many times before I was ten
I walked with my grandfather like a man
From Richmond to Kingston beside the Thames.

And looking back at the White Cross Hotel
Which D.H. Lawrence must have had in mind
(I thought years later) in *The Rainbow*,
And at Water Lane
Where fishermen must once have disembarked,
He'd tell me how
Mainly before the war but much less now,
Poor people from the East End would come down
On the District or the old North London Line
To spend a Sunday, their one day free.
And I'd look at the ground
And think of the shoes poor people wore,
And we would keep on walking.

And two miles on he'd always pause
To single out a certain clump of trees.
And while I'd stare at the unremarkable clump
Which looked like all the other clumps, he'd say
'Before the war, there was a very nasty murder here.
And do you know, they never found him.'

And at Teddington Lock
Beyond which was the One Mile Tree
(Which meant another fifteen minutes
And then a wait for the 65 or 71)
He'd remark, smiling rather, yet astounded, on the day
A German bomb fell smack into the Thames,
And fish, bigger than anyone imagined there could be,
Still less there, in grubby Thames,
Floated up, stone dead.
'Best thing Jerry ever did, giving us those fish.'

And once he said, just once,
As if to himself, as if I were too young to hear,
'Just as well they didn't win the war.
It'd be bad enough for me,
But as for you...'

And as I looked at the sky, the river,
And at him, and at my own bare knees,
And at my smart leather Start-Rite sandals
Done up tight but comfortably,
I suddenly knew what a small boy I was.

And I wondered for years
As the Thames rolled down to London
And beyond.

The Blind (by Pieter Breughel the Younger, 1638)

Osiers there are, perhaps a lake
Whose blue is blue as Breughel's sky.

But what is that to them,
The two men unexplained of middle age
Whose red of coat and stocking gleams
In dusk or dawn against the marshy ground
Where one leans on the other's shoulder blades
And he with fingers curved against the shock
Of what is real or not at all
Tests step by step mysterious paths of air?

After Work

Other men in raincoats would appear
Around the corner, disillusioning
Because they were not you.
As they passed the stonemason's yard
Where the concrete angel stood for years
And the private detective's always
Locked (its blinds pulled down: we never saw the man),
I'd grow impatient for your sombre-coated form
And leather case that authorised the day
As evening now. Although I knew
So far away you couldn't see me wave,
The moment that you came in sight I'd wave
And wave, and keep on waving as you neared.

How strange that forty years from then,
Those other men, not you, so long ago
Dismissed as disappointments to a small boy's eyes,
Come trudging,
Tired, perhaps, but quickening their step
Past the angel's frozen sprinkling pose,
Past the office with the blinds all drawn,
Homeward through my grown-up mind
That now will never know the mysteries
Of welcome or of solitude they walked towards
Those early twilights through suburban streets.

Pencil

Consider how this slender rod of stone,
So tightly packed, uncracking, into wood,
Passes through your days unmarvelled at until
With eyes two inches from the moving point you see
The unsuspected alchemy unique to form

As yours the needling beck aslant the slate,
The tributaries, rapids, cataracts,
Or water-meadow-flanked meanders, ox bow lakes,
The swallow-skimmed, the spreading depths…

And then to shape,
Beyond all these, and very faint,
The graphite darkly lustrous in its layers
Beneath the earth unmined,
And some forgotten tree.

Beneath a Grubby Sky

The runway, after all, proved long enough,
And as the plane cleaves skyward, he winds down,
At pains to camouflage overt relief,
And notes a fresh astonishment of sun
That moulds the clouds, to him, most fittingly
His own beside the tunnelled paid-for calm:
This spreading nonchalance of magazines,
The trolley-guiding smile in place, the wine
In plastic glass, the peanuts' oiliness.
Beyond, the blue-white freedom beckons him
In oval miniatures epitomised
As if by Hilliard now become Magritte.
'World is mad, madder than we realise,'
Once more he muses as he's borne to where
A gramophone is floating in a swamp
And playing *Spem in Alium*, ignored
By dunlin, auks, anhingas, mastodons.

Awakening at last to roaring dark
He finds his fear transformed, to his disquiet,
Without his stir, into bewilderment
Towards those random passengers who share
With him by numbered chance these seven hours
To sit unscreaming in their rigid chairs
And gawp at screened utopias, or peer
At laptops in arthritic attitudes
With just – at this he blanches, almost shouts –
This strip-lit tube of gas on fire
To case them from the height-thinned freezing air
Or, far beneath, the breakers' ice-smashed trawl.

His wristwatch off, his mobile phone stuffed deep
Into his bag, beneath his socks, he stalks
Through immigration, customs, not as one
Noise-hammered into jetlagged unbelief
But as himself now, lucidly enthralled.
And now, while others dash to car or train,
He contemplates outlandish buildings, sky,
And long inhales a different country's air.
In time he'll take a bus to anywhere
Whose name he rather likes, whose shops and streets,
Suburban, seedy, unexceptional,
He'll potter in, anonymous, unknown.
There, rather as a man who signs his will,
Entrusts the copy to its drawer, then pours
A tawny double Scotch, he sees himself
With condescension's pleasing pity stroll
From filofax and phone so neatly packed
Into a gauzy plastic bag. But now
It pleases him, beneath a grubby sky
Portending slanting rain, to muse upon
The concrete roads and car-exhausted air.
He takes his time. He likes to take his time.
He knows he'll live by wonder now, by whim,
His clouded days lit up by hidden sun.

Scientific Proof

As a child he tested God
With radishes.

Two rows he planted –
One to be blessed,
One to be cursed.

And when both thrived alike
He knew the truth
And never thought again –

Until in age,
Renowned, deceived –

About his childish test of God
And radishes identical in rows.

Even This

Yet even this becomes too much.
Ten times at least, she called him just to say
'I love you'
On his answering machine. And he,
Having drunk too many beers
And in accordance somewhat more than usual
On guard, on guard against impetuosity,
Heard, as well, the uninflected formula
Of statement, phrase, then time of day or night,
Of that tireless woman he would never meet,
Who never would make love to him
Or drive a car right down his drive and have him
Starting from his desk, hands waggling as a high-strung child.
And then, between the times intoned,
The other one kept saying
'I love you.'
Wearying, he sought for variation there
(Music faint but recognizable, perhaps King Oliver),
But none there was, just the voice
Pronouncing unrelievedly
'I love you'
At him undressing now for bed,
Rather sadly, hoping for the best.

Musings in Amsterdam

Down from Ben Cohen's on the Rozengracht,
A coot is nesting on a sunken boat
While by the water's edge a cage of wire
Is failing to retain a wall of bricks
Beneath a shattered sign that read, I think,
Tabasco once. With hypodermic stretch
A heron damply treads a balcony.
Above, apartments reach six storeys high,
Abandoned, near the roofs, to birds and rain.

What envy draws me to the edge of things:
The playing fields at twilight just before
The groundsman casts one last misgiving look
Towards the toilets' dulled Edwardian brick,
Then clangs the iron gates shut? Or else that street
Of blackened houses by the factories
Where net was perishing behind the glass
And where, lost thirty years ago as now,
I noticed as I cycled up and down
As if I had some destination, how,
Half-lit by filmy bulb, a woman seemed
To move within, and wait, and somehow knew.

And even now, perhaps, five storeys high,
Beneath an unwashed pane aslant towards
The shifting geography of sky, a girl,
Fey-slovenly, while reading Stefan Zweig
Might wonder how it feels to live,
A generation on, with mobile phones,
The emptiness, if emptiness it is,
Of Olga Korbut's afternoons. Perhaps,
But better that she sit imagined there
Both ever and yet never to be met
By me in daydreams on a public bench
Down from Ben Cohen's on the Rozengracht,
In fears that love themselves yet shirk all risk.

Him

His toylike plough comes charging past my door
With him atop it, fifty-five but driving like a boy,
Exuberant in orange jacket, woolly hat.

There fell a foot or more of snow last night.
I'm idling over coffee, unconcerned
About my shifted day.

But he's still at it in my drive, beavering away –
Forward, then abrupt reverse
As if he must erase both snow and earth.

This April it will be two years, I muse.

Now he's hammering my neighbour's drive beneath
A leaden sky inert with snow.

Corridor

(for Sandy Marovitz)

My colleagues daub their office doors
With posters, aphorisms, comic strips,
Or children's drawings in wax crayon.

For thirty years his door's stood plain,
As just itself: the grain,
And eight small letters of his name.

Three Views from the Age of 45

I

Thirty years ahead
On days it's warm enough to sit outside
To muse upon the lilacs and the flower beds
And groundsel thriving in between the flags,
What could be more bludgeoning
Than thinking all the very things
That one day, thirty years ago,
You had identified as those
You'd hate to think you would be thinking
Thirty years ahead?

II

'Mistakes are all there, waiting to be made,'
A man named Tartakower said, of chess.
By extension, this is all I know
Of how to live the life that's left.

III

I would like to bask all afternoon
On an old bench
With a nice cat.

Falling

We children thought our school would fall
Although it never did, although we knew
It was the clouds behind that moved.

I'd squeal and thrill, and ape to flee
The thunderous crashing of Victorian brick
But in due course forgot the school that fell,
And moving falling anything at all

Until this morning, writing at my desk,
I chanced to see amid sun-sculpted clouds
The moon go sliding down the sky to earth,
And realised how much of life I'd lost.

A View of Clumber Park

My mother painted, twenty years ago,
A watercolour view of Clumber Park, near Nottingham.
Or rather, I should say,
Its pleasing honey-coloured ironstone bridge.

Well, yes…
But what I longed for in that vast expanse
Of water in the foreground was

Rhinoceros.

You need to have him horning left to right,
Iridescent sapling-green and on the slant,
For, as Picasso wrote,
No one pays attention to what's straight.

We need much more of him,
Much more of him, again I say,
In art and everything:

Rhinoceros!

Evening in the Playing Fields

'He played for England in the seventies,'
One of their fathers passingly remarked.
But to the scatter of small boys who dash
Towards the goals he's just that weird grown-up
Who's always at it where they want to play,
Alone and shooting at an empty net.

How well they know his ritual: the ball
Spun wristily into the fingertips
And placed with what might pass for tenderness
Upon the spot (precisely on the spot –
It must not budge from where it's put: the spot)
And then the sternly-paced-out yards to where
Undeafened by catcalling fans whose jeers,
Whose jeers might cause a weaker man to err
And fluff his kick, he thinks his action through
From run to swing to high up to the left
Beyond the reach of any flailing glove
Of any keeper in the world – then shoots.

Now many hours have passed. The boys are gone.
But on the pitch the damp is on the rise
As still he pauses, sets his furrowed sights
At gallows, ghostly in the fading light,
Then thunders unrelenting in to make
The leather pay for thirty years ago.
The street lamps gleam. To him the poplars stand
As dark as magistrates around the ground
To judge alike and unforgivingly
The soft assenting swish of net or else
The drilled or wafted silences, and ring
His self-contracted nine yards' strip of world
With no one left to care, as ball by ball,
He strikes with wild atonement at the past.

Once, over twenty years ago, in France…

Owl

At times when owl, and only owl, will do,
How enormously I'd like to read
A poem named 'The Owl' or 'Owl'
To put me well in mind of one,
Grave or astonished of eye
Or in half-slumber in some ancient tree.

How marvellous a word it is:
Owl.
I can see it owling at me now.

But every time I'm promised owl I read
Of war, or nerve-storms, states of mind
Of lonely men unloved
In which the owl, if owl there be at all,
Is incidental.

I want him to be central,
Central.

Is it much I ask?

Hecceity

Now *this,*
This is where the whole damned lot makes sense:
The contract starts to write itself, and all across the Middle East
Beggars rise as one and buy themselves
Armani suits,
– And just before the sun –
As in the hothouse now the mercury
Is on the rise
– And just before the sun –
I slow myself to think of that most magnificent word,

Hecceity

Which four centuries ago Sir Thomas Urquhart coined to mean
The quality of something being this
– And now the sun, the great gesticulating bastard sun
Comes crashing in its thisness through,
And all the world's umbrellas, all in me,
Open and close and open and close and open and close.

Mrs Claus

Consider creatures as were born in fire
Or ash, the half-lion half-man manticore,
Or else conceived by sun in muddy banks
Or thriving jewel-eyed in the rotting hearts
Of century-old oaks! How quaint these seem,
Consigned to fable, woodcut, analect,
And yet this Mrs Claus, who year by year
Proclaims the very insecurities
That gave her birth, prodigious stands at ease
As fear and dogma's mismatched masterpiece.

Well Alone

Iridescent on the shore,
The stone was taken,
Varnished,
Set to catch the light.

Someone took the poem
Gouged deep into its crumpled page,
Smoothed its edges,
Gave it sheen, elan.

Was the stone then not a stone?
Was the poem anything at all?

Autobiography in 1958

You are two years old.
You are sitting on an air raid shelter
At the end of your grandparents' garden.
The concrete is hot.

Your parents are in New York for a year.
They write you letters with American stamps.
But they will come back, you know they will,
To see you being three.

At night you sometimes dream that you're on board
A long dark train. But daylight comes.
You know that daylight always comes.
You know it does.

There and Here

In England, outlines blur:
Church, hill,
Village, pub and field

Are smudged, bruised
By cities
Crowding in.

But here the roads go on and on and on
Through the cities,
Making light of them.

And beyond,
Beneath the purging sky,
Run unfenced empty roads

As if in its entirety the buzzard-circled world
Were yours
And free.